The Sailor Who Drank The Sea

Marcel Martinez

BookLeaf Publishing

India | USA | UK

Presentation by *BookLeaf Publishing*

Web: www.bookleafpub.com

E-mail: info@bookleafpub.com

ISBN: 978-93-5744-362-3

First edition 2022

Fall

Crashing waterfalls
Sunken under the waves
Watching the rainbow

REminder

Memories replaced
Colorless they became
A reminder resulted in forced laughter
                    Laughter
                    laughter, a
reminder resulted in broken vaults
                    Rainbows sprung
from the heartstrings
                    Makeup faded,
revealing the lacerations

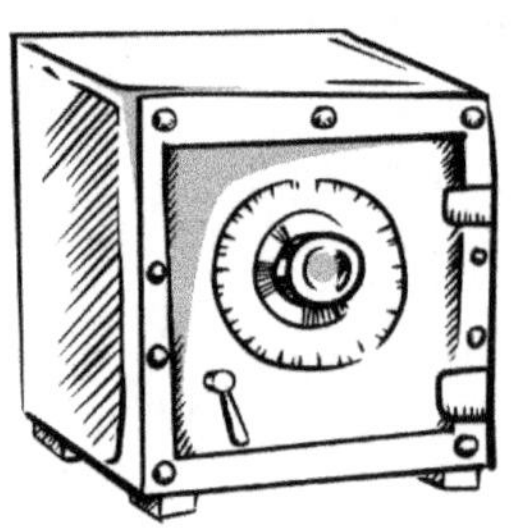

REopened

Comfort in the constraints
Gifts from his unpolished hands
Produced torn ribbons
The book only carried one page
Yet eyes stuck to it like velcro
Ripping became bothersome music
Deafening horns
Again and Again
Madness.
Red rosary dangled from his palms
The veneer of the faceless
Born with a cup half empty
Hoping for it to fill

REflection

Split
Enticing sideshow
Lifeless mirrors, there might be a smile
For the empty reflection
Inside or out?
Strikes continue to tally regardless
Hopefully the reflection smiles back

Solemn underneath the surface
More f.looding
In no time
Love begins to crack
Everything will be ok

A Mosaic

Crushed glass
A reflection bouncing about
Cuts and bruises faced the mirrors
A canvas that once was
Clear as diamonds
Now colored like a mosaic

In The Hurricane

Fear in an ocean of sorrows
Might pulled the steer in the face of the
blistering winds
The rigorous showers doused the survivors
Waves thrashing against the hull
Hope slipping through their blistered palms
Eyelids pressed tightly like a hug of infancy
Fully expecting damnation
The eye opened
Revealing the spotlight

It Never Entered My Mind

Crashing waves
Her smile blocked the sun
But the shade was fine between her dimples
Sand stuck between velvet toenails
A poor reflection of what sat behind the wax
An unbearable inferno that burned without
regret
The only result was love letters in the rain
Her spirit, similar to the blissful winds in
autumn
Allowing the dead leaves to dance once again
The only regret was the sleepless nights
What remained was nothing but cold charcoal
May the cold see this fire spark again

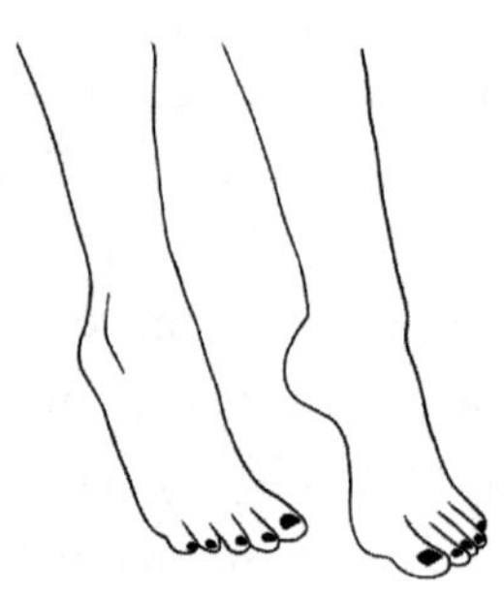

Drowning

Most things are strong enough to surface after the waves. But others get swallowed whole within the warm waters. Drowning in the ocean of pain. Drowning in the ocean of solitude. Drowning with many others, although the water remained thick enough to separate. But diving in was from my own hands, so why? Why do I find regret within the decision? The saltwater isn't so bad for the wounds though. The mass of self-inflicted wounds that mask the gash from another. Slowly plummeting into death's grip. Slowly declining to the dark abyss. Nothing but hollow glass remained within the sand. Sand stained with blood. From me? Or from former comrades? Whatever it may be, the waves swallowed everything whole. Vision began to dwindle into black. Squeezed tightly like limes for the sweet waves. Inhaled deeply by the lethal current. It left nothing but a smile on death's surface. The difference was cloudy at the bottom of the barrel.

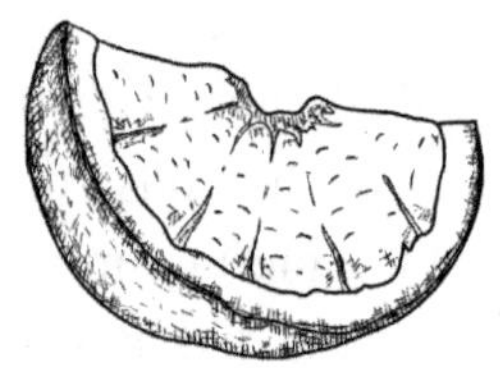

Still waters

sAt silently
reflecting the moon
stars shined Violently against the reflection
the lone sailor stood Envious of the mirrors
Men can only wish to sing such a fine melody
maybe one day
the voiceless will no longer be mutE

In The Sea Of

Sitting on the empty sunkissed dock was an occupied war torn wooden sailboat. It wasn't anything more than that, but the one occupying it cherished it dearly. A sailor prepared for whatever journeys the sailboat allowed him to. Seeing the black sand beaches of the west or even possibly the pink waves of the east. Whatever beautiful sights sat in tomorrows crosshairs, the sailor anticipated nothing short of adventure. The only drawback to the fantastic fire that sat in the heart of the sailor was the tired sailboat. Did it have anything left in it to set sail once again? After many travels it shared with the sailor, the signs of experience began to show. The sailor knew of the handicap that cursed the sailboat, but adventure was the only thing in his heart.

a reoccurring colour

thundershowers oFten stRuck the silent Oceans
at night
claps loud enough to aMass the canvas into new
shades
how often do These new shades come without
invitation?
only the creatures beneatH the current could
predict the future
and yet
Eden was a much more alluring picture

While Yesterday

The wreckage costs the sailor dearly. The snow-tipped mountain tops were nothing more than a pipe dream. Maybe reality was no longer needed for the sailor who stood in agony from losing himself. The ship became hazy and the ocean became black. Why was the past taken for granted? Only the sailor knew that pipe dreams produced sewage. Maybe that was where he belonged. Tattoos of yesterday stained his sleeves with blood. Tomorrow shall take its time.

became colorless

forgiveness
it was More exclusive
than the fOuntain of youth
and yet
you sat there, askiNg for it
even after
the countless Sins
that sTained your hands
you stood there, without an ouncE of shame
or Rather
without a face

Where time became numb

Sitting on an empty colorless dock was an occupied war-torn sailor. The scars from battle left him in solitude, as the image only became grotesque. A sailor without a sailboat who enjoyed grey skies in the rain. Was another day without the sea worth waiting for? The smell of lavender incense burns against the borders. The memories were left behind like footprints in the snow. A man without purpose was dead weight. Were fantasies of premature finales worth another song?

Solitude even lost its taste. The thoughts slowly faded to routine. Another being without a fingerprint. Why were the days losing a grip of their worth?

i am loved

i am loved
i am loved
i am loved
i am loved.

a burning fire seared the man who hung from the clouds.

Drifting away on a new raft
This was the man's return from hiatus
The sea salt finally returned to the ocean
In it, fish swam underneath the clear surface
The fires burned brightly, glowing like the sun
The dreams were soon to be in tomorrows hands
Days no longer came without the colors of the
sunset

smiling isn't so bad

flowers danced under the sun
colors saturated brightly into the palette
the sun shined on the canvas
its reflection created silhouettes that appeared
like stars
only so many things made the painter smile
it made him believe there were no such thing as
a meaningless sight

Winter

the sea was flavorless no more
reminiscent of the breaths that weren't visible in
the winter
remembering the nights where the only company
you had was the water
but now
the waves no longer carried the foggy tint of
mahogany
while the scars began to wash away under the
waterfall
it could be some time before the moon shows
enjoy the rainbows while they last

The Line Between Boys and Men

What differentiates boys from men?
My old man always said the hair
on your upper lip makes you
a man. But i thought that it was the will
to be the mature and wise one
rather than getting caught up in ego.

But is it ego
That makes one turn into a man?
Grandpa told me the one
who chooses to go without their hair
is the one who will
always prosper, you

should always follow your
dreams and fulfill the dreams of others, not your
ego.
But who actually, willingly
Goes for their dreams? Not a man
in my house, it was more of the facial hair
that held the line between the boys and the ones

Who weren't so. But that one

thing, is that enough, even after you,
yourself grow facial hair
and choose the path of dreams after being
blinded by ego.
But i still felt i was not a man,
but will

that makes me a man, will
it! Even though i still felt i was the one
who was sitting upon the line between boys and
men.
Even after you've
graduated through the school of egoism
and shaved every last strand of hair

On your head. Only the hair
On your upper lip remains. Do i have the will
to actually bare my face without hair
for the one
life that will truly make you
a man?

Three Words In A Bottle

40

It was I who was responsible for my own
undoing
Even then, love still remained as elusive as
dragonflies
sitting exposed, my broken bones came with no
casts
Will the self finally be capitalized in selfish?

3

The Sailor Who Drank The Sea

I didn't always find attraction in the sailor's knot
And there once was a time where the skies were blue
Might it be that I've become accustomed to the concrete
For that always came with everything it promised
Rainy days made it a beautiful sight
Every spot sparkled against the streetlights
Even then, how could I forget the clouds?